Permission to Be an Artist

Reframing the Boundaries
of the Elite Art World

Megan Auman

Copyright © 2023 by Megan Auman

All images copyright © 2023 Megan Auman

All rights reserved.

No part of this book may be reproduced without the author's consent.

*For Mom,
who showed me how to be an artist.*

*And for anyone who has ever felt like what
they make doesn't qualify as art, or who has
ever struggled to call themselves an artist.*

Table of Contents

Identity 5

Value 17

Education 37

Location 53

Labor 79

Permission 95

    Acknowledgments 109

    Selected Bibliography 113

    About the Author 117

"State that painting is a high art, furniture making a craft, and you instill in a culture an inborn preference in its creative individuals to reach for a brush and canvas rather than a saw and a plank of wood."
-Hugh Moss

"…you have to know your history to understand how to challenge its legacy."
-Alice Proctor

Identity

Artist. Few words bring up such complex meanings and emotions. It is a definition, an identity, a joy, and, some might say, a curse. It is applied specifically, to a certain kind of role or career, or broadly, as a way to highlight skill, creativity, or virtuosity in just about any field. There are people who want to protect the term artist, make it imply a certain level of skill and professionalism, like doctor or lawyer, and those who proclaim everyone is an artist.

For my part, I fall somewhere in the middle. I don't believe everyone is an artist, which is not to say that I don't believe that everyone has the capacity to be an artist, but that not everyone is because not

Identity

everyone chooses to be. I think of it the same way I think of athletes or musicians or any of the other wonderful endeavors our human bodies are capable of doing. We all have the capacity, to varying degrees, but we don't all choose to do all of these things. And just like I believe that you don't have to win a gold medal to be an athlete, you don't need to have your work in the Louvre, or any other museum for that matter, to be an artist.

Artist, athlete, musician: these are identities we get to bestow upon ourselves and we get to claim them, if we so choose, regardless of education, status, or awards. But of course, there are those that disagree.

These days, I am apt to describe myself as an artist and metalsmith. (Also a teacher and writer, but those are conversations for other books.) Ironically, I struggled for years to commit to those two titles - artist and metalsmith - despite literally having a piece of paper that confers upon me the degree of Bachelor of Fine Arts in Metalsmithing. Geez, how

Identity

twisted is it that I couldn't claim the titles that came with my diploma?!? And if someone who has not one but two degrees in art struggles with these things, how are those who didn't go through the university system supposed to feel?

I don't have to guess. I know. After working with countless creatives, many of whom don't have a degree in art, I've seen every level of hesitancy when it comes to claiming the banner of artist. Like me, many dance around the title, identifying as makers, designers, or creatives, or they lean into their particular material or process, calling themselves a potter or a weaver.

There is nothing wrong with any of these terms and please continue using them if they have meaning to you. But there's also something about calling yourself an artist, or being called an artist by others, that just feels different.

Chances are, if you picked up this book, you feel that pull, even if you can't quite explain why.

Identity

Ultimately, there are two main reasons to take on the title of artist instead of, or in addition to, one of the many other ways you could identify yourself.

The first is value. Like it or not, we code things labeled as art as more valuable than things we think of as craft or just generally, stuff. If you're trying to make a living from what you make, this designation has real implications for your ability to do so, starting with the value others place on your work and the prices you can charge for it.

While the first reason to identify as an artist - value - is external, the second - permission - is internal. There is a creative freedom that comes from being an artist, a mindset and attitude that allows us to approach the world differently. When you identify as an artist, you can "get away" with all kinds of things. I've had people proclaim "she's an artist" as justification for a range of my activities, from dying my hair bright pink to collecting copious amounts of shells on a beach with my friend's daughter to lingering a little longer than most while looking at

Identity

art. I could describe countless other behaviors that my art has justified, but at the end of the day, artists just seem to move through the world in a different way.

Unfortunately, the reasons that many of us don't view ourselves as artists aren't only in our heads. They are the result of real cultural programming, dating back centuries, that tells us that certain types of creative output are art and others aren't. If, as I did, you went to art school, you probably absorbed a great deal of this programming. It might have been implied, or it might have been explicitly stated. It might have even fucked with your head like it did mine.

Art school, even in wonderfully supportive programs like the ones I attended, has this uncanny ability to plant seeds of doubt at every step. Maybe it's the endless critiques - when you know your work will be ripped apart at the end, occasionally literally, but mostly metaphorically, you start questioning what you're making before it

Identity

even comes into being. And it's not a far cry to go from questioning your work - asking, "Is it even art?" - to wondering if you are worthy of being called an artist. So much time is spent doubting in art school that it's easy to get turned upside down, to get lost as to who an artist even is, to wonder if you deserve that mantle.

But prior to art school, it was so clear to me who an artist was. I knew because I lived with one.

My mother was so many things in her life - daughter, sister, wife, mother, aunt, friend, lifeguard, synchronized swimmer, bird watcher, bowler, step aerobics devotee (at least during the 90s) - but the identity that held the greatest sway on myself and my siblings was artist. Whenever we had to list my mother's occupation on a form growing up, we wrote artist. This in spite of the fact that, to my knowledge, my mother never sold a piece of her art. Nor, as far as I know, did she desire to. I never asked.

Identity

Not that it mattered. Artist was such a core part of my mother's identity that of course we - my siblings and I - considered it her occupation. And it was. After her family, nothing occupied my mother's time and attention as much as art.

From the time I was young, my mother was devoted to her weekly painting class, a commitment she kept even after adding three more children to the mix and even after being diagnosed with cancer. But her weekly classes and regular workshops weren't the only times she made art: our home was filled with works in progress, not to mention an ever-expanding collection of art books, reflecting her insatiable desire to learn new techniques and processes. Her finished art filled our home, though she was quick to give her art away as gifts to friends, family, and her children's teachers. Even now, years after her death, I run into acquaintances who tell me with pride about the art she made them and how they still display it in their homes.

Identity

I wish I could list my occupation as artist with that same certainty. I waver, sometimes writing self-employed or business owner, but in my more confident moments, writing artist. My accountant lists my profession as artist on my taxes, which must count for something.

My mother's path to art was completely different from mine. She studied psychology in college. But she did take at least one art survey course. I have her textbook, *Varieties of Visual Experience*. It sits in my studio, alongside her picture, several of her paintings, a container of her paintbrushes, and a few trinkets she brought back for me from her trip to Paris - tiny perfume bottles and a little statuette of the Eiffel Tower.

Whether you went to art school or not, you're likely not immune to feelings of fear and doubt about whether or not you deserve to call yourself an artist. To this day, I wonder how my mother escaped those doubts. Or maybe she had them, she just never imparted them to her children.

Identity

Which is honestly one of the greatest gifts a mother can give.

Our thoughts - what we believe to be true and false about ourselves and our identities - don't just spring out of nothing. They are a complicated web of the social and cultural patterns that came before us. Some were imprinted from our families, some from our friends, and some from the cultural zeitgeist.

The boundaries the art world has created have trickled into our broader world, in ways many of us don't even realize. Nowhere is this more true than in the story of who does and doesn't get to call themselves an artist. Art world elitism, the art/craft divide, the gender and racial disparity in museums - all of these have deep historical roots, some of which I unpack and explore in this book.

But this book is more than just history. It comes from my own lived experience as an artist, someone who has worked in a variety of materials,

Identity

and at various times has either proudly claimed the title, felt guilt over thinking it belonged to me, or abandoned it altogether in favor of "safer" labels like designer or creative.

This is my exploration of what it means to be an artist and how that identity sits within the broader history of the art world. My hope is that in my story and my examination of the history of what it means to be called an artist, you'll see glimpses of yourself, and that you'll start to unpack your own patterns of hesitancy and self-doubt.

Ultimately, regardless of your creative output, by the end of this book, I want you to claim the title of artist.

Not because I told you, in no uncertain terms, that you should. But because you were able to unpack all the bullshit reasons that you thought you couldn't. Because you understand that it isn't some mental or emotional shortcoming that prevents you from taking on that mantle. Because you know

Identity

that your self-doubt isn't self-made. It comes from centuries of institutional and cultural boundaries. And because you understand that calling yourself an artist is truly one of the most radical things you can do in the face of that cultural programming.

Value

In the early days of the pandemic, a survey out of Singapore named artist as the number one non-essential job.

Despite its small sample size - only 1000 people - the survey ignited outrage in my online circles. "Who do they think creates all those movies they've been watching or the patterns on their bougie pajamas?" people posted angrily in comments and DMs. "Where do they think the pictures on all those puzzles they've been doing come from?" Still, others took it to heart. Who were we to continue making art, of doing something so apparently non-essential, in the face of human suffering?

Value

Unfortunately, it doesn't take cataclysmic events to feel doubt about the value of making art. It's quite common.

The most memorable moment for me came at the start of my final year of graduate school. I had the opportunity to attend a workshop at the Penland School of Craft, in the Appalachian Mountains of North Carolina, to study with an artist I admired. It should have been a dream, making art in this prestigious and naturally stunning setting. Yet somehow I was miserable, plagued with self-doubt. *What was I doing with my life? Why did it even matter?* The pressure of it became too much, and one afternoon I left the metals studio, breaking into a run in the woods in my jeans and studio apron. Panting, hands on my knees, I tried fathoming any other more valuable life plan, and when I couldn't come up with a viable alternative, I pulled myself together and headed back to the studio, still heavy with doubt.

Value

Most artists I know have a similar experience, some moment where they felt like their work was for nothing. Being an artist is to be constantly plagued with self-doubt. Not just "Is my work any good?" but "Why does it, why does art, even matter?"

If calling yourself an artist comes with so much self-doubt, why would anyone want to claim that title?

Because the alternative is even worse.

If art has the potential to be pointless, frivolous, non-essential, what about the things that can't even be classified as art? What about all the other stuff, the detritus of our modern world? That is even less than worthless, as the Capital A art world is apt to remind those of us that don't fit into their ever-shifting, yet somehow rigidly defined boundaries. We run the risk of being labeled "just a crafter" or "only an illustrator" or, that greatest of Modernist insults, making work that is "merely decorative," that can't even be classified as "real" art.

Value

Being an artist may come with its own set of problems, but standing outside the art world, looking in through the window while the world around you goes to hell is a special kind of torture.

This feeling, that many of us who make things are on the outside looking in, is by design. In her book *Painting Professionals*, historian Kirsten Swinth argues persuasively that our modern art market, with its elite gallery system, was created to stop the perceived parity that women were gaining with men in the art world. In reality, women artists made up just over 30% of the exhibitors in the old system of juried shows that dominated the second half of the nineteenth century in America, but apparently, that was too much. The gallery system arose to give men (white men, to be clear) an advantage over their female colleagues. And the gallery system did its job. In the early years of the twentieth century, women made up only 7% of the artists exhibiting in galleries.[1]

---

[1] Kirsten Swinth, *Painting Professionals*, Chapel Hill: The University of North Carolina Press, 2001.

A century later, the numbers are not much better. According to one report, women accounted for only 27% of solo shows in galleries in the US, despite making up 51% of working visual artists.[2] The picture is also bleak for artists of color and LGBTQIA+ artists, who make up far less of the artists represented in galleries, museums, and auctions than they do the general population.

For all the myths and jokes about starving artists, the reality is that there is real money and power within the elite art world. This means the stakes are high for keeping some people at the top while also clinging to any precarious sense of value in the art market. This winner takes all strategy assumes that to keep the value (read: the price) high for certain types of art, other types must not only be excluded but denigrated. And it's not just certain types of art. Certain types of people, who don't fit the prescribed mold, must also be excluded. Thus, we

---

[2] Rebecca Wilson, "How the $760 Billion Art Industry Could Change if Women Were Given Equal Exposure," *Observer*, observer.com, February 10, 2020.

get not only systems but also writing and criticism, that maintain certain types of creatives aren't real artists at all.

This is the point in this book where it would be helpful if I gave you my definition of art. Something clear-cut, so we were all on the same page. But I'm not sure I can do that. For centuries, I daresay millennia, philosophers of all stripes have been trying to identify a universal definition of art. But universal definitions are hard to come by. Art plays a role in almost every culture around the globe and throughout our history as a people, but it doesn't look the same everywhere, and not every culture has a word for what English-speaking people call art.

If I was hard-pressed, I would probably define art as something made by humans to make us feel something. But oh, if that isn't such a vague description as to be practically useless.

Value

Feeling stuck and still without a concrete definition of art, I take a break from writing and head to the bookstore. Midtown Scholar in Harrisburg has the largest section of art books I've seen outside a museum gift shop or Strand Books in New York City, which makes it one of my happy places. I'm thinking about how we define art when a book in the Folk Art section catches my eye. *Home-Made Europe* is a collection of photographs of one-off objects made by hand, along with the names and stories of the creators, as collected by the author, Vladimir Arkhipov. There are chairs, all sorts of tools, a tent, a bag to carry gâteau - a word I recognize as being French for cake, thanks to the silly little app I'm using to pretend I'm learning French - and a dildo carved from stone that a woman made to keep herself satisfied while in prison. (This is one of the few entries that doesn't include a full name or picture of the creator.) All the items in the book have a wonderfully inventive air about them, a satisfying combination of imagination and ingenuity.

Value

A universal definition of art may be hard to come by, but there's no denying the number of categories that have been created to designate art with a capital A (translation: art approved by the Euro-patriarchal capitalist art complex) from other art. Folk art, outsider art, decorative art, craft: the boundaries between these areas are loose, something I ponder as I try to figure out how books on craftswomen of the world, a Japanese basketmaker, and a collection of watercolor illustrations of early Colonial American art all ended up in Folk Art instead of Decorative Art or Art & Craft. I'm glad I'm not the one who has to sort and shelve these books, but at the same time, I want to scoop them up in my arms, mix them up, and throw away these arbitrary boundaries.

A book called *Russian Folk Art* catches my eye on the crowded shelf. Russian art holds a special place for me. When I was fourteen, the summer before my sophomore year of high school, my mother took me and my eleven-year-old sister on an artist exchange trip to Russia.[3] Most of the women on the trip - and they were all women, except for two boys, the same age as my sister and me, who came with their mothers - were there because they had taken painting classes with a group of Russian artists who visited the United States the previous year.

The trip took us from major cities - Moscow, St. Petersburg - with stunning palaces and museums - the Hermitage, Peterhof - to small towns - Tver, Palekh - where artists worked in collective shops painting decorative trays and little lacquered boxes. This was in 1996, and the artists needed to get creative now that their workshops were no longer supported by the Communist state. In the case of the artists we met, it was a combination of

---

[3] I have chosen to include the story of my trip to Russia in this book because it was influential in my development as an artist and a person. This should in no way be taken as an endorsement of current Russian foreign policy. I stand in solidarity with the people of Ukraine against Russia's unlawful invasion of their country.

traveling to teach and creating work for the tourist trade that paid the bills.

It never occurred to me, in my young, optimistic, pre-art school state, that there was any difference between the rural artists we met and any other kind of artist. Sure, some artists might be more famous than others, but they were all artists. During the school year following our trip, I had to write a term paper for my World Cultures class, and in my youthful pretension, I wrote it on the state of the arts in post-Communist Russia. I don't have that paper anymore, though I wish I did, (except I don't because it's probably terrible) but I do remember that I wrote about Russian Constructivists and the communities of rural artists we met on our travels with the same level of attention. As far as I was concerned, every artist in Russia was in the same boat.

Sadly, the art world proper doesn't see it this way. While the boundaries between folk art, decorative art, and craft may be fluid, the boundary between these areas and capital A art is more rigidly policed. Like anything that has its roots in Euro-patriarchal culture, money and power lie at the heart of the issue.

Our modern distinctions between fine and decorative art have their roots in the Renaissance when painters and sculptors hoped to elevate their trade beyond the base, bodily world of the manual arts towards the realm of the brain and intellect. The painter or sculptor was no longer a craftsman, defined by a particular skill, but a *thinking man*, defined by his ideas. (And yes, I'm using masculine pronouns intentionally here, because while there were certainly female artists during the Renaissance, the elevation of the brain over the body was a thinly veiled attempt to elevate the masculine over the feminine, not to mention an attempt to distinguish Western European people from the cultures they were beginning to colonize.)

This separation was easy to maintain while painting and sculpture focused on representation, but the development of abstraction in the early twentieth century came with a new problem. How to distinguish abstract painting from all the surface decoration and pattern that heretofore had not counted as real art? And more importantly, how to ensure that those abstract paintings were valued at a much higher price than their decorative counterparts?

Enter Clement Greenberg.

There are many in the art world for whom Greenberg still serves as a kind of hero, the high priest of Modernism, but in this story, Greenberg is one of the villains. Best known for his 1939 essay "Avant-Garde and Kitsch" and his championing of Abstract Expressionism in general and Jackson Pollock in particular, many of the ideas Greenberg espoused are still circulating in the art world some twenty-five years after his death.

"Avant-Garde and Kitsch" set the stage for many of the divisions between art and mass culture that we still see today, but it was Greenberg's later writing where he truly sowed the seeds of division. In his criticism, Greenberg frequently evoked the term "decorative," and other words related to craft and decoration, as pejoratives. In her essay "The Decorative, Abstraction, and the Hierarchy of Art and Craft in the Art Criticism of Clement Greenberg," Elissa Auther refers to Greenberg's use of the verb "embroiders" in his review of the paintings of Morris Graves. She writes, "The real bite in Greenberg's critique derives from the classification of needlecraft as a popular art form, one, in fact, that is practiced almost exclusively by women... This type of artistic production, although labour intensive and often of a high skill level, is easily dismissed as uncreative, derivative, and a display of craftsmanship as an end in itself."[4]

Like any skilled manipulator, Greenberg's digs are subtle. He doesn't state outright that decoration or

---

[4] Elissa Auther, "The Decorative, Abstraction, and the Hierarchy of Art and Craft in the Art Criticism of Clement Greenberg," Oxford Art Journal, Vol. 27, No. 3, 2004.

domestic art is bad. Even in "Avant-Garde and Kitsch," he pays lip service to folk art, trying to differentiate it from the mass-produced culture he defines as kitsch. But what he does instead, using terms like "merely decorative" or "embroidered" to denigrate work he doesn't like, is just as insidious. It reinforces a culture where art made for the home, art that employs decorative motifs, art typically made by women or people of color, is valued less, if it's even considered art at all.

Greenberg died in 1994, but his ideas about what does and doesn't constitute art still loom large. I can point to two recent incidents that remind me that, at least in some places, those rigid art world hierarchies are still alive and well.

In his book *The Death of the Artist,* William Deresiewicz examines the ways the Internet is impacting our ability to make a living from our art. In the chapter on the visual arts, he notes that while artists, in general, are struggling, the Internet has opened up new opportunities to make money in fields such as "illustration, cartooning, graphic design, and crafts." But he then goes on to say, "The question for all of these creative forms, however... is whether they are art."[5] These words sting, and next to that paragraph, in my copy, I've scrawled a note: "Ugh, fuck you." This is not the first time I've written something similar in the margins of this book. I mark the point where I can no longer stomach his ideas with the note "elitist prick," close the book, and proceed to rant about it in an Instagram video.

"Well, what did you expect from a book called *The Death of the Artist*?" someone remarks in response to my frustration. Honestly, my hopes were higher. I vigorously agreed with an earlier chapter, "Art and Money," enthusiastically underlining and starring whole passages. I thought that Deresiewicz might be a kindred spirit, aware of the challenges - but also maybe the opportunities - that the Internet age has provided for artists of all stripes. What I

---

[5] William Deresiewicz, *The Death of the Artist*, New York: Henry Holt, 2020.

didn't expect was for Deresiewicz to employ the type of art world gatekeeping that has been happening for decades, centuries really, the kind of gatekeeping that I first became aware of in art school, the kind that says certain types of creatives are artists but others aren't.

Another place I didn't expect to hear this kind of dated gatekeeping was on a podcast with marketing expert Seth Godin. I have long been a fan of Godin, hearing him speak in person and referencing him in my first book, so this one stung. Speaking on the Art Juice podcast, Godin throws digs at "decorative" that are straight out of the Greenberg-ian playbook. This isn't speculation. Godin name-drops Greenberg in the episode while taking a condescending and patronizing tone toward the type of work that is being created by a lot of the podcast's potential listeners.

Just like with Deresiewicz, I shouldn't have been surprised. The title of the episode is "Are You a Painter or an Artist?" Still, it bothered me to hear someone I had previously respected spouting such elitist art world bullshit.

Obviously, I don't believe the artificial boundaries imposed by the art world that say some of us make art, and some of us, because of material choice, format, gender, race, nationality, or some other factor, do not. If I did, I wouldn't be writing this book.

But I know there are many artists, or those who dream of being artists, who will listen to that interview and doubt the value of what they do. They will worry that they are "merely a painter" and not fit to take on the mantle of artist, with any hope of the value or prestige that could come with that title.

You might be wondering, why does this matter? Who cares if some writer thinks painters and sculptors are artists but illustrators and crafters are not? Why does it matter if you're considered an artist or "merely" a painter? Who cares if I write "artist" or "self-employed" on government documents?

I read a stat recently that says we discard most of our stuff within six months of receiving it, which is of course an ecological nightmare. At its core, art is one of the few categories of things we still consider special. I'm not saying art never ends up at the thrift shop or in the landfill. That would be the height of hubris. But we tend to value the things we call art more. We keep them, we care for them, we delight in their presence.

In his book *Emotionally Durable Design*, Jonathan Chapman argues that "waste is nothing more than a symptom of a failed relationship."[6] Most of the things we buy end up in a landfill because they do not engage with us in the long term. Most things do not require "the degree of care, focus, and

---

[6] Jonathan Chapman, *Emotionally Durable Design*, Oxfordshire: Routledge, 2015.

overall emotional involvement"[7] to keep us around for the long haul. But art, which I vaguely defined as something made by humans with the goal of making us feel something, has the potential to do this, to provide a more meaningful and less fleeting experience.

For anyone who aspires to sell the work they make, there is one other value piece at play here. Not only do we tend to treasure things coded as art, but we tend to pay more for them in the first place. There's no doubt that calling something art gives the price tag a boost in the way that calling it craft or handmade does not. In a business that often operates with razor-thin margins, the value difference between claiming something is art and claiming that it's one of the "other" categories can be massive.

Even if we're still a bit fuzzy on the definition of art, there is one inarguable fact. Art is made by artists.

---

[7] Ibid.

Value

If we limit who can be considered an artist, we certainly limit what is considered art and what we value as art.

But those limits - between capital A art and all the "other" arts: folk, outsider, craft, decorative, et al - don't exist for good reasons. I would argue they exist for the very worst reasons - to marginalize and devalue the things made by certain groups of people.

To claim the title of artist - particularly if you fall into a group or category that's historically been devalued - is a powerful act of resistance. It's to claim a value for your work that, for many of us, we weren't historically granted. To say you are an artist is to say that you create something meaningful, something worth keeping.

Education

At some point in my junior year of high school, I decided I was going to go to art school. Or rather, I decided I was going to go to school for art. I had been dancing around it for a while - after cycling through the normal girlhood desire to be a teacher and a marine biologist, I decided I wanted to be an architect. I asked my dad to bring me home graph paper from work - owning a machine shop, he had plenty to spare - and I set about imagining my future career. But at some point, I decided that I had only chosen architecture because it felt practical. What I really wanted to go to school for, I told my parents decisively, was painting.

Fortunately, my parents were nothing but supportive, at least outwardly. They paid for me to

Education

attend a four-week summer program at the University of the Arts between my junior and senior years (I did manage to get a partial scholarship, but I still know the program wasn't cheap) and my mom drove me to an interview for an arts magnet program that let me leave my high school halfway through the day to take art classes at the local community college.

Their support in my decision to become a painter was unwavering, but I could feel my dad let out a sigh of relief when I came home from the community college one day that fall and declared that I had again changed my mind. As part of the arts magnet program, we spent Friday afternoons immersed in various disciplines outside of our main drawing and 2D design classes. The community college had an incredible range of materials and processes including a full glass hot shop - one reason I was interested in the program - and we got to experiment with many of them. We had already tackled lithography (not really my jam) before moving on to create lost-wax cast silver

Education

rings. "You can go to college for THIS?!?" I remember thinking. "Sign me up!"

Wanting to encourage what he saw as the more economically viable option, my dad arranged for me to visit a local jeweler and spend some time at his bench. He also, one Sunday morning, drove me to Syracuse - a school I had only applied to because they happened to have a metalsmithing major, but who had offered me a rather large scholarship - to look around.

I've told this story - of how I went on to get my BFA in Metalsmithing, and then, because I didn't know what to do with it, I got an MFA for good measure - more times than I can count. That feeling - of discovering in my senior year of high school something that so clearly lit me up and that would inform my life's trajectory for the next twenty-plus years - makes for great interview fodder, especially on a podcast.

Education

I always tell the story as if it is miraculous. And in some ways it is. I work with artists and makers all the time who don't discover their passion for art - whether that's art in general or a specific medium - until much later in life. I also meet so many artists and makers who knew early on that they wanted to pursue art, but financial and practical concerns, or family disdain, meant that wasn't an option. For those people, I am one of the lucky ones, who was able to chase her dream from an early age.

But on the flip side, my story isn't miraculous at all. It's the story of a white girl from a financially privileged background, whose parents paid for her to go to college, and because she didn't have to take on any debt until graduate school, was free to pursue something that had no guarantee of financial return. That makes me, even now, the type of person most likely to earn a degree in art. Because it turns out that material privilege, more than passion or interest, is the biggest factor in whether or not someone studies art in college.

Education

Actually, it's the biggest factor in whether or not someone can pursue art at all, whether formally or informally. Plunk my family's financial situation down into many other times in history and the results probably would have been similar. I might not have gone to art school - because art school is a more recent phenomenon - but I likely would have had the financial resources to pursue art, even if only as an avocation.

My story isn't miraculous in the context of our current world, but it is in the long history of art. For most of the history of the world, artists weren't trained in colleges or universities at all. This is one of those things that, if you think about it, makes the idea that you can only call yourself an artist if you went to art school even more bullshit.

A quick Google search yields the following facts: One of the earliest art schools was founded in Paris in 1682. The oldest art school in the US, the Pennsylvania Academy of Fine Arts, was founded in 1805. Another article tells me that "the first true academy for art instruction"[8] was founded in Florence in 1563, though you could only become a member if you were already a recognized artist.

This isn't exactly what we have in mind when we talk about art school, though you could argue that the portfolio requirements of many art programs also require you to "be an artist" before you go to school to become an artist. This is the situation I found myself in when I applied to art school. Besides my high school art classes, I had taken workshops with my mom's painting teacher, completed a four-week summer program at the University of the Arts in Philly, where I focused on drawing, painting, and sculpting from the figure, and took life drawing and 2D design classes at my local community college, all in service of creating a portfolio to get me into the art programs of my choosing.

---

[8] Editors of Encyclopedia Britannica, "academy of art," britannica.com, February 9, 2023.

Education

"You should have taken shop classes," my husband likes to joke about my art school experience, where I spent most of my time working with tools that more closely resembled his time in high school shop class, rather than what I created in my high school art classes.

"I didn't have time," I always reply. "I needed to take drawing and painting to build the portfolio that would get me into art school." This was a portfolio that harkened back to the early days of the art academy, full of life drawings, because the ability to draw the human figure from life was considered the ultimate skill. Though as a woman, at certain points in history, I would have been barred from drawing the nude from life. If I was lucky, I could have studied from plaster casts or eventually, I could have enrolled in a teacher training program that allowed me to study art, or enrolled in a graphic arts program to become a commercial artist, both of which made up the career path of Georgia O'Keeffe.

Education

As someone who attended art school and taught art at the university level, I often find myself thinking of the role that art schools and university programs play in the development of artists. And my bookshelves reflect that, as I've accumulated many books over the years about the history and theory of art at the collegiate level. Struggling to find one of the books I'm sure I own (but not sure where I've placed it), I search for it on Amazon to confirm the title. I'm a little surprised when I see the first line of the description for *Art Subjects: Making Artists in the American University* by Howard Singerman bluntly states "Nearly every artist under the age of fifty in the United States today has a Master of Fine Arts degree."[9]

That can't be true, I think to myself. Especially when you factor in that this book was published in 1999. Does that mean that now, almost every artist under the age of 70 has an MFA?

---

[9] product description for Howard Singerman, *Art Subjects: Making Artists in the American University,* amazon.com, viewed June 26, 2023

I once again turn to Google, where the results are a little murky, at best. Part of the problem is in how you define an artist, and every article or study has its own methodology. A 2016 report by the group BFAMFAPhD argues that "40 percent of working artists do not have bachelor's degrees in any field"[10] but their research includes writers, actors, musicians, and more, in addition to those working in the visual arts. In an article on Artnet, researchers looked at the top 500 living artists born after 1966 based on Artnet's own sales data and concluded that 53% had an MFA, 35% had a degree but not an MFA, and 12% were "self-taught" meaning they had no degree in art.[11] While this group in no way represents the broadest range of those working as artists today, and the BFAMFAPhD study is practically too broad, neither seems to support the assertion that "nearly every artist under the age of

---

[10] Susan Jahoda, Blair Murphy, Vicky Virgin, and Caroline Woolard, "Artists Report Back: A National Study on the Lives of Art Graduates and Working Artists," BFAMFAPhD, 2014.

[11] Ben Davis, "Is Getting an MFA Worth the Price?" *Artnet*, artnet.com, August 30, 2016.

fifty in the United States today has a Master of Fine Arts degree."

I'm fascinated by the use of the phrase "self-taught" in Artnet's article to reference artists without a degree, even if those artists did attend some art school. It speaks to how pervasive the idea of a university degree as the only true path to learning art has become in our society. Yet, as I mentioned before, in the grand history of art, university art programs are a relatively recent phenomenon. And the idea of "self-taught" is a red herring, meant to bolster the ideals of the university while degrading all other forms of learning.

This is understandable. Universities have to justify their existence and a lot of time, energy, and money have gone into creating university-based art programs. But it's important to look at who benefits when one type of learning is valued and others are denigrated.

Education

In a 2023 commencement address at Smith College, activist and writer Reshma Saujani takes to task the idea of imposter syndrome. Referencing an Atlantic article by Leslie Jamison, Saujani shares the origins of this idea, which wasn't originally coded a "syndrome" at all but rather a phenomenon. I've long harbored the idea that imposter syndrome is bullshit, but I've never quite been able to verbalize why until I watched Saujani's speech on Instagram.

"When as many as 82% of women report feeling imposter syndrome," Saujani states, "it's hard to believe this is just about individuals. Imposter syndrome is the result of structural inequality, not individual inadequacy."[12]

She goes on, "It's never been about whether we're qualified enough, smart enough, prepared enough... Instead, it's always been about the

---

[12] "Imposter Syndrome Is A Scheme: Reshma Saujani's Smith College Commencement Address," YouTube.com, viewed June 26, 2023.

political, the financial, the cultural barriers that are designed to keep us out of these rooms in the first place."[13]

There have been times in its brief history when the art school has had more democratic aims. Normal schools sought to create teachers skilled in the arts so they could bring those skills to the youth in American schools. Learning to draw was seen as a form of moral virtue. But for the most part, art schools and university art programs always skewed elite. They were there not for everyone, but for people who looked like me - white and privileged, with family money that kept the school's coffers in good shape.

This is one of the main reasons that, despite pervasive sexism, art schools and programs were often largely made up of women. Referring to American art schools in the nineteenth century, Kirsten Swinth writes, "Lacking the government

---

[13] Ibid.

Education

patronage of their European counterparts, American schools depended on women students for their fees. At base, that meant they needed women for their financial survival."[14]

But women's presence in art school didn't increase their perception as legitimate artists. Swinth also writes, "The growing numbers of women art students and artists spurred and intensified the move to professionalism by men who sought to use professional standards to enhance their own status and delegitimize others in pursuit of 'amateur accomplishments.'"[15] The proliferation of art schools and universities granting degrees was a direct result of the desire to professionalize art, in an attempt to reward some practitioners and marginalize others.

The first BFA and MFA degrees were established at

---

[14] Kirsten Swinth, *Painting Professionals*, Chapel Hill: The University of North Carolina Press, 2001.

[15] Ibid.

Education

the University of Iowa in 1938, and yet somehow, in the last 85 years, we have come to believe (or more accurately, been led to believe) that this is the standard and legitimate way to become an artist, all other methods be damned. But in the history of art and humanity, this is merely a blip, and it's possible that's all it will be. I don't regret my time in art school for one moment, but as the costs of a university education continue to rise, I find myself questioning the idea of art school as the only route to becoming an artist.

For those that didn't go to art school, your feelings of inadequacy are by design. But that doesn't make them necessary. As Saujuni says, "Imposter syndrome is a distraction, it's a strategy. It's a way to keep our concentration on our own alleged inadequacies so we don't turn it towards the sexism, the racism, the classism, the homophobia, the transphobia that is baked into the system in the first place."[16] All of these things are baked into the elite art world and the world of higher education, just like they're baked into our society.

It's up to us, as artists, regardless of how or where we learned to do what we do, to let go of these alleged inadequacies, so that we can stake our claim to the art world, to declare that an artist isn't made in an art school, that there are so many paths to becoming one.

I tell my story - of discovering metalsmithing, choosing it as my college major, and getting two degrees - as miraculous because it is. Despite what the description for Singerman's book would have us believe, I am the exception, not the rule. There is not a single, respectable path to becoming an artist, and it's time we stop believing otherwise.

---

[16] "Imposter Syndrome Is A Scheme: Reshma Saujani's Smith College Commencement Address," YouTube.com, viewed June 26, 2023.

Location

The first work of art that really moved me was Salvador Dalí's "Last Supper" at the National Gallery of Art in Washington, D.C. When I was a teenager, that painting hung on a landing in the middle of two escalators that transported you from the old building to the underground tunnel that led to the new wing. I say transported because that's how I felt seeing the painting for the first time. Standing on the escalator as it moved downward, the painting slowly revealed itself, little by little, until you were struck by the massive image of Christ floating in the sky. The experience of not having to walk towards the painting, but rather being carried, as if I too was floating, left me stunned. For the rest of my teenage years, anytime we took a field trip to D.C. (not an uncommon occurrence when you grow up just a few hours away in central Pennsylvania), I made a point to visit that painting. Riding the escalator towards it, on tenterhooks for it to appear, that painting never failed to astonish me.

Only a few other moments in my life have matched that experience: the first time I read an excerpt from Annie Dillard's *Holy the Firm* in my high school English class - sitting there, eyes wide, disbelieving that such magic could exist in written form and that somehow, my classmates couldn't see it; touring Frank Lloyd Wright's Taliesin West, held rapt as our guide spun tales of grandeur in the Arizona desert; an exhibition at the Metropolitan Museum of Art of eighteenth-century French clothing installed in rooms of the same period - which made my heart ache with the beauty of it all; and a spellbinding Sunday morning in Milan, where I saw Leonardo DaVinci's Last Supper - a much more gratifying painting to see in person than the Mona Lisa, its ghostly images practically floating from the wall, calling me back towards another time - and then found myself utterly alone on the roof of the Duomo for what felt like a breathless eternity.

On my last visit to the National Gallery of Art several years ago, I was disappointed to discover that the Dalí painting had been moved from its perch on that landing. Now, or at least as of my last trip, the painting hangs in the newer, modern wing on a wall that juts out at an awkward angle across from a bank of elevators. It is still technically impressive, and its strange positioning might be more appropriate for a work of Surrealism, but sadly, the original enchantment is gone.

While I still believe in the power of a work of art to move me - the sight of a Diebenkorn at SFMOMA a few years ago brought me to tears - it seems that some of the allure of Dalí's Last Supper was literally in how I approached the work, and not in the work itself. Still, I haven't given up searching for that particular high that comes from being blown away by a work of art.

Location

And I'm not alone.

In the year before the pandemic, the world's 100 most popular art museums received an estimated 230 million visitors.[17] Even with museums closed for much of the year, those same museums still received 53 million visitors in 2020.

I daresay that when pressed to describe a memorable encounter with art, most people will describe an experience like mine. A work of art, often of epic proportions, in a museum or gallery; maybe a blockbuster exhibition, Alexander McQueen at the Met comes to mind; or perhaps even a monument or work of architecture.

For most people, this is their experience of art. Art, at least "real" art, is something that we view away from our everyday lives. We travel and seek it out. It

---

[17] Emily Sharpe and José da Silva, "Visitor Figures 2020: top 100 art museums revealed as attendance drops by 77% worldwide," *The Art Newspaper*, theartnewspaper.com, March 31, 2021.

Location

is powerful, moving, awe-inspiring, but also fleeting. In their book *Art as Therapy*, Alain de Botton and John Armstrong write that art "is a therapeutic medium that can help guide, exhort, and console its viewers, enabling them to become better versions of themselves."[18] Noble goals, but difficult to actualize if the only art we encounter is locked away in museums and galleries. A painting we see once a year or once in a lifetime is unlikely to be a salve for our everyday troubles.

This was never so clear to me as it was during the pandemic, when stuck in my house and unable to visit the museums I love, I decided to repaint the set of stairs that lead from my second-floor studio down to the garage where I keep my torches. (The welding process I use for my jewelry is too dirty to keep in my main studio.) As would be expected from a secondary staircase that leads to a garage, this was a pretty sad affair. Just blank walls and

---

[18] Alain de Botton and John Armstrong, *Art as Therapy*, London: Phaidon Press, 2016.

Location

bare steps, since I had pulled off the dirty old mauve carpet years ago.

Inspired by the book *Joyful*, I decided to paint the stairs (not the walls, the stairs themselves) in a graduated set of teal blues, with a pop of coral at the top. I was about a third of the way up the stairs, happily painting away, when it hit me.

I had spent so much of my life chasing the high of museums. Not just visiting them, but dreaming that someday, *someday,* I might make something worthy of being in one. I mean, that's the height of what it means to be an artist, right? That someday, you'll create something that someone wants to keep forever, perfectly enshrined in a temperature-controlled gallery.

But suddenly, at that moment, I realized I had gotten it all wrong. The most important art isn't the art in museums. It's the art we live with, each and every day.

Location

From that perspective, it's probably safe to say that I interact with more art in the first hour of my day than many people do in twenty-four hours.

It starts with my water glass, or more accurately, my water mug. Handmade by an artist in Seattle, the mug is cream stoneware with denim blue leaves, at times bold and other times delicate, stems and buds reaching gently upwards, emerging from the surface. Stout and sturdy, this mug became my water mug by default, because I couldn't bear the thought of staining that creamy surface with tea. But in truth, I love the feel of it in my hand - the weight of it, the texture - and the way it looks - fueling my hunger for pattern - and so I want to keep it close throughout my day, like a comforting talisman.

The first half-hour or so of my day is spent reading. While some people chose to spend their mornings outside enjoying nature or hit the gym for a sweat session before work, I prefer to ease into my day in the company of books and art. With my mug by my

Location

side, I settle into my well-worn spot on the living room sofa. If my eyes wander from my book, they are likely to land on the bookcase in front of me. The lower two shelves, tilted from years of too much weight, are given over to books, but the upper three shelves hold art.

On the upper two shelves sit a pair of prints that I picked up as part of a larger set at a craft show ages ago: sepia ink on tan paper, one with a crow in a thicket of brambles, the other a crane among cattails. Next to one of those prints is a smaller work of art - red-tail hawk feathers meticulously carved out of layers of paint, their texture extending down below a faded teal surface - and a ceramic pitcher covered with a pattern resembling a geometric quilt in shades of turquoise and aqua. On the shelf below that is another small painting, this one full of abstract shapes, splotches of ultramarine, creamy peach, and blush pink that carry over to the edges of the white canvas, and floating amongst all of that, one leaf, resembling a monstera more than anything else, quickly

Location

rendered in indigo ink. In front of the painting is a small ceramic planter. The planter itself is commercially made, but my mother painted the surface to resemble a lily pond by way of Claude Monet. A small pothos grows from the pot, a cutting I took from a plant my mother gave my brother many years ago, a plant he miraculously managed to keep alive through several moves, a marriage, and two small children.

The bookshelf leans against a narrow stretch of wall between a window and the fireplace. On the windowsill are a set of ceramic cups, pale porcelain with delicate lines scratched into the surface in shades of lemon and lilac, that I've turned into planters. From the fireplace mantel hang fabric pinecones, made by folding squares of fabric into even smaller squares and pinning them to styrofoam eggs. I made most of these myself, sitting on a couch with my mother during the last Christmas season of her life. We made those pinecones like women possessed, grateful for something to pass the time, for an activity that my mother could do in her weakened state. Seeing these pinecones never makes me sad. Instead, they fill me with gratitude for that final winter spent with her. Next to the pinecones hangs a wreath made from grey felt roses, accented by a solitary white rose, sent to me by the seller education team at Etsy as condolence after my mother's death. Like the pinecones, the wreath's presence is not a constant reminder of grief, but rather of the love and support I received during a difficult time.

I could continue like this, highlighting the art in other parts of my living room or perhaps in the dining room where I sit typing this, my next destination after reading on the couch. I could go on and on about the art around me, the art that fills my home and studio, the art in my wardrobe. But I want to stop for a moment, because depending on who you are - your education, your background, your point of view - you may not believe that most of what I've been describing to you is art. Sure, the paintings might count, perhaps the prints. But the mugs, the painted planter, the wreath, the fabric

Location

pinecones? For some people, it's a stretch to call those things art.

Like so much of the language that surrounds the idea of capital A art, this is by design. Yes, we're back to that old chestnut - the art/craft divide. Thanks to a healthy dose of patriarchy and racism that grew out of the Renaissance and the Enlightenment, we've been taught that certain media and certain processes constitute art, while others are simply craft, made not by artists, but by artisans or craftspeople or - and this word can carry so much disdain from both the establishment and the general public - crafters.

But there's something also at play here - the very location of the work itself. We're taught to believe that great art, *real art,* doesn't aspire to end up in someone's home. We're taught that the goal of art, and thus the goal of artists, is to end up in a museum.

Location

In an essay originally written for the World Craft Council, poet and critic Octavio Paz treads on well-worn distinctions between art, craft, and design by viewing the relationship each has to time. Art, Paz argues, aspires to be timeless, bound for "the air-conditioned eternity of the museum."[19] Design, the work of industry, meanwhile, is fated to end up in the trash bin. (Though of course, we can all name "iconic" examples of design that have ended up in museums.) Of the three, craft alone operates on human time.

Paz writes, "Craftsmanship does not aspire to last for millennia, but at the same time it seeks no early death. It follows the course of time from day to day, it flows along with it us… the work of craftsmanship is the pulse of human time."[20]

---

[19] Octavio Paz, "Seeing and Using: Art and Craftsmanship" from *Convergences: Essays on Art and Literature*, San Diego: Harcourt Brace Jovanovich, Inc, 1987.

[20] Ibid.

Location

I'll admit that I find this beautiful, this relationship of craft to a lifetime. But I also feel the need to point out that most of the "timeless" art only remains so because a team of very skilled conservators works very hard to keep it that way. Much of the art in our museums was, just like the work that Paz calls craft, not meant to last that long.

So what makes the museum the ultimate aspiration for art? Paz argues it is the way that art evolved from religion. "Art inherited from the old religion the power of consecrating things and endowing them with a sort of eternity; museums are our temples and the objects displayed in them are beyond history."[21]

Paz is not the only one to make this connection between art and religion. In her book *The Whole Picture*, Alice Proctor writes, "…museums have often been compared to shrines, spaces that command a kind of adoration… Architecturally,

---

[21] Ibid.

Location

they frequently resemble temples."[22] Emerging from a tradition of religious artifacts, museums have replaced churches as the site for venerating objects.

But this doesn't give the full picture of why art intended for the home is often not considered art at all. Before we dive into the more modern history, I think it's worth noting that this wasn't always the case. In the history of humankind, museums, just like art schools, are a fairly recent invention. It is only since the seventeenth century that the museum as we know it has existed. Prior to that, all objects that we now consider art were made for one of two purposes: religious or domestic. Art was a part of ritual or it was a part of daily life. (And sometimes, it was both.) Even the earliest museums grew out of collections that originated in the home, though most of these homes were owned by incredibly wealthy individuals.

---

[22] Alice Proctor, *The Whole Picture: The Colonial History of Art in Our Museums*, London: Cassell, 2020.

Location

The home as a location for art had its moments even after the creation of the museum. Impressionists like Monet were not opposed to their work ending up in homes, though of course, those homes belonged to wealthy collectors. And the Arts & Craft Movement, spearheaded by William Morris, sought to integrate art into every element of domestic life. (Again, most of the works made by Morris & Co. were available only to the wealthy, though I would argue that is a by-product of the labor inherent in the decorative aesthetic of Arts & Crafts designs, rather than the sole intent of the work.)

No, to understand why art for the home isn't viewed as art, we have to return to Clement Greenberg and his friends, the (male) Abstract Expressionists. After Greenberg's 1939 essay "Avant-Garde and Kitsch" asserted that the avant-garde belonged in the gallery while the site of kitsch was the home, the Abstract Expressionists were only too happy to take up the charge, creating oversized paintings that blatantly rejected the domestic sphere. And this wasn't just assumed. In the introduction to *Not at Home: The Suppression of Domesticity in Modern Art and Architecture*, editor Christopher Reed shares a quote from Robert Motherwell, "The large format, at one blow, destroyed the century-long tendency of the French to domesticate modern painting, to make it intimate."[23]

And there you have it. In a few short decades, the lines were drawn. Big things were for the gallery and the museum, and small, intimate things were for the home. And these small things were not art, they were, in the eyes of Greenberg and his contemporaries, kitsch, mass culture, or "merely decorative."

It's also important to acknowledge that the epic art Motherwell described - made for the gallery or museum - is not just a modern convention, it's a

---

[23] Christopher Reed, *Not at Home: The Suppression of Domesticity in Modern Art and Architecture*, London: Thames and Hudson, 1996.

Location

Western one as well. Writing about Chinese art, Hugh Moss notes "Paintings evolved from walls and screens (and room dividers) to more intimate formats such as hanging scrolls, hand scrolls, albums and fans - all formats that could be picked up and handled… The art that mattered to this sophisticated aesthetic culture was intimate and private, made on a manageable scale."[24]

When I left graduate school, I found myself at a bit of a crossroads in my relationship with the big = museums, small = domestic equation. In the three years it took to complete my MFA, I balanced two bodies of work with very different goals. While I started off making large wearable pieces (I called them jewelry, but for many, that would be a stretch), by my second year, I had made the transition to sculpture. I had a few reasons for this. The first was simply that the scale I was working in had started to become cumbersome for wearable work. The second was that I wanted to use my time

---

[24] Hugh Moss, *The Art of Understanding Art: A New Perspective,* London: Profile Books, 2015.

Location

in art school to make things that were completely impractical. I figured that I had the rest of my career to make more "commercial" work if that was what I chose. But the third reason, if we're being completely honest, is that I wanted to make things that felt worthy of a place in a gallery and maybe even one day, a museum.

At the same time, I was also an active participant in our program's jewelry student co-op. The goal of the co-op was to help prepare students for a future selling their work, typically as production jewelers. Participation was optional, but students were encouraged to submit pieces for our biannual student jewelry sales. As someone who has always been fascinated with business (I launched my first one in fourth grade, selling handmade confetti to my classmates) I took the co-op just as seriously as I took my studio work and by the time I left graduate school, I had a fairly well fleshed out production line, ready to take to sell to the masses. (I'm being ironic here: by masses, I mean the people attending the one retail craft show I did that summer in Northeast Ohio.)

In my first year after graduate school, I continued to balance these two lines. I was teaching at a university full time, and I knew, if I wanted to continue in academia, I needed to continue to make work that was worthy of gallery exhibitions, for it was this, rather than proof of my pedagogical skills, that would land me better teaching jobs. But I also continued to develop my production line and launched my Etsy shop in the same year.

Eventually, I found my desire to run my own business and have control of my time was stronger than my desire to stay in academia and I left to focus on the world of retail craft shows and selling wholesale to stores. With that decision, I stopped making the large-scale sculptures that had landed me several gallery shows to focus on my production jewelry line.

Location

Simply put, I chose to make work for everyday life, not for the museum.

At their worst, museums are deeply problematic, filled with stolen artifacts (yes, I know, they aren't all stolen) and reflecting racist and sexist ideologies. But at their best, they're democratic, allowing the public access to incredible works of art. I'm grateful for the beautiful objects that end up in museums because if they lived solely with wealthy collectors, I, and so many others, would never have the chance to experience them.

And there's nothing wrong with aspiring to have your work in a museum if that's your goal. I'll admit that I still harbor that fantasy for my work, a dream I'll probably carry until the day I die.

But I also understand that the ultimate goal of a work of art doesn't have to be a museum and that something doesn't have to be in a museum to be a work of art. As Alice Proctor puts it, "Don't fall into the complacency of believing that, if it's worthy, it is

Location

in a museum - and conversely, if it's not in the museum, it's not relevant."[25]

Still, there's no denying that museums seem to offer a sense of validation.

In 2018, the Metropolitan Museum of Art launched a landmark exhibition "Jewelry: The Body Adorned." Despite living a two-and-a-half-ish hour drive from the Met, depending on traffic, I see that exhibition five times in its not-quite four-month run. I go with friends, trying not to influence their viewing too much, but secretly hoping they too gravitate toward my favorite pieces. But mostly, I go alone. I linger over gold bracelets, with stones rising triumphantly in their settings, and marvel that these pieces, made during the Byzantine era some 1500 years ago, have survived all this time. That the worth of them as objects, as adornment, as art, has somehow triumphed over their value as raw materials. I dip low and bring my face as close

---

[25] Alice Proctor, *The Whole Picture: The Colonial History of Art in Our Museums*, London: Cassell, 2020.

Location

to the glass as feels allowable, trying to see a gorgeous copper Art Smith collar from every angle, to know how the hinge works, how he utilized metalsmithing skills that were so simple, yet so efficient and masterful.

I go, and I feel grateful. The exhibition serves as empirical proof that the subject, the topic, the thing I've devoted the last twenty-plus years of my life to - longer if you count childhood friendship bracelets and weavings on my bead loom - is not without meaning, not superficial or devoid of value.

But I also feel a little disappointed. Because despite its subtitle, "The Body Transformed," the body feels strangely absent from this exhibition. Sure, there are some images of jewelry being worn; a few African sculptures adorned with necklaces; a dancing Hindu deity carved from stone and dripping with jewelry rendered in the same material as the statue's body; and, in an attempt to elicit a whiff of scandal, an old

Location

fashioned peep show box featuring a Victorian woman reclining nude. But overall, the exhibition is about the objects, not the body.

When I think of the objects in the exhibition, most not intended to spend their lives in museums, but rather to be worn, celebrated, and cherished, I think of the movie *Toy Story 2*. Feeling less than loved by his owner Andy, a cowboy doll named Woody contemplates joining a few other toys from his heyday as they are prepared for a toy museum in Japan. The price for immortality is a lifetime enclosed in glass, forever admired by children, but never touched, or arguably, loved, again. It is only when a rescue party arrives, in the form of Andy's other toys, that Woody realizes it is better to be loved deeply, to be played with, held by a single child, and run the risk of ruin or abandonment, than to live forever behind glass.

Do the pieces of jewelry in the museum feel this way? Do they see me pressed against the glass and long to feel the touch of flesh, to nestle in the curve of a bosom, to hang precariously from an ear?

Jewelry doesn't feel, though I would pay to see that Pixar movie - a bracelet, lost from her owner, or perhaps an earring, missing her mate - even if it would surely leave me in a blubbering heap by the end. Jewelry doesn't feel, but bodies do. I do. I feel, and I feel a sense of longing that I can only know each of these gorgeous pieces of jewelry through a wall of glass.

And this is the disservice we create when we think art only exists for the museum. We deprive people of the immediate, sensory pleasure of art in their everyday lives.

It's likely that most of us who make things will eventually have to make a choice: between pursuing work that is destined for a museum and creating work that is intended to be used (and potentially, in the words of Octavio Paz, used up) in real life.

Location

Despite what Greenberg and his ilk would have us believe, one isn't any more art than the other, and choosing to make work for everyday life, for the home and the people who live in it, doesn't make you any less of an artist. I would even argue the opposite. Because as I realized in those early days of lockdown, an inkling that started as I toured the Met's jewelry exhibition and dreamed of wearing the work on display, the most valuable art - the art that has the capacity to change us - isn't the art that resides in museums. It's the art we live with every single day that truly has the ability to impact our lives.

Labor

In a show of works by the late artist Etel Adnan at the Guggenheim in New York, a pair of shimmering textiles catch my eye. It could be the scale. They are significantly larger than anything else in the show. But no, that's not it. It's the striation of color, the way that one mass blends and fades into the next. Like color field paintings, except that the color is literally woven into the surface.

I spend an inordinate amount of time staring at these tapestries, trying to understand how they are made. I press myself as close to the wall as I can without physically touching it - or drawing the ire of the guards - to try and see the other side.

Labor

In truth, I know how these are made. They are woven on a tapestry loom by skilled makers who weave each color into place individually. They are made slowly - one area, one thread at a time. I know this, but it doesn't make them any less magical, at least to me.

My friend has a different opinion. "They were my least favorite thing in the show," she tells me when we compare notes, "because she didn't actually make them."

And it's true. Adnan created the designs for these pieces - known in the industry as cartoons - and then contracted with a weaving workshop to have them produced. But to me, that doesn't make them any less masterful. These pieces are the epitome of collaboration, an artist whose vision was executed by a team of some would say artisans, but I would equally call them artists. The visual acuity and skill needed to blend those colors in such a glorious way is as much an art as creating a painting, even if the weavers remain uncredited.

Labor

I'm reminded of these tapestries when a glass artist brings up a question in the forums of my online mentorship program. As someone who routinely exhibits at high-end art and craft fairs, she wonders if it's ok to have a line of work that is made solely by assistants. She worries about drawing the ire of other exhibiting artists, some of whom, in a Facebook group she belongs to, are quick to take to task the work of "production houses" who exhibit and win awards at shows that are supposedly just for artists.

There's a part of me that is over these conversations that seem to resurface every few years and which are surely rehashed more often in Facebook groups in which I no longer participate. But I understand why they continue.

The question of who makes the work has been a source of anxiety for artists - and those who wish to be called artists - for years. It's particularly true for artists who work in media traditionally labeled as craft. Starting in the 80s, craft tried (some would argue in vain) to be seen more seriously as fine art. That meant adopting the posturing of the art world, including the myth of the artist as solitary genius.

When I think of the origins of the artist as solitary genius myth, I picture Jackson Pollock, slinging paint in his barn in the Hamptons. But in her insightful book *Monsters: A Fan's Dilemma*, Claire Dederer takes it back to Pablo Picasso. (Though she too references Pollock.) She writes," The genius is the one who is able to exert control over his materials and his helpers while simultaneously *absolutely* losing control over himself."[26] The genius, alone in his studio, is wild and free. (And, as Dederer points out, always male.)

In the 2018 documentary, *The Price of Everything*, filmmaker Nathaniel Kahn takes us on an exploration of value in the contemporary art market through interviews with collectors and

---

[26] Claire Dederer, *Monsters: A Fan's Dilemma*, London: Scepter, 2023

Labor

artists, many of whom share their process for the camera. While the film showcases the work of a range of artists, it's hard not to view it as the story of two - Jeff Koons and Larry Poons - and even harder not to view Poons as the winner, the more likable and triumphant artist at the end.

Throughout the film, both men are shown in their studios. Koons' is a massive New York City loft where assistants sit behind him, dutifully painting and enacting his various projects. By contrast, Poons is shown mostly alone (though occasionally with his wife), working in his studio in a dilapidated barn in upstate New York.

Koons is the art-world manipulator, fawning for the camera and touting his genius while his beleaguered employees do the work behind him. Poons is the heroic figure, fiendishly working in his barn in a legacy that owes much to the mythic images and videos of Pollock throwing paint on the floor, except Poons' canvas is tacked loosely to the wall, enveloping most of the room in a circle of frenetic paint.

To be fair, it is as much Koons' personality as his method of producing art that makes him the villain. He is smarmy and self-centered, whereas Poons is reflective and mostly good-spirited about his fall from the art-world spotlight after his style shifted from his best-known Pop Art of the 60s. Even when he ribs a curator for complimenting his early work but not his more recent pieces, he does so without malice or spite.

Despite the fact that Koons has a net worth from his art sales that is twenty or forty times higher than Poons (depending on which source you believe) it is the image of Poons, and his solitary painting in the barn, that we tend to view as the "authentic" artist. Or maybe that discrepancy in sales is why. Poons is a real artist, whereas Koons is a capitalist opportunist. He was, after all, a Wall Street broker before making his move to art, as the film aptly reminds us when it intersperses an interview with Koons with a clip from The Wolf of Wall Street.

Selling art, or selling a lot of your art, doesn't automatically make you a greedy capitalist. (A phrase which, now that I've written it, smacks of redundancy. Aren't capitalists, by their very nature, required to be greedy? Isn't that how capitalism works?) Instead, I'm reminded of a recent New Yorker article I read on the problems with A.I. The author, Ted Chiang writes, "When I refer to capitalism, I'm not talking about the exchange of goods or services for prices determined by a market, which is a property of many economic systems…whenever I criticize capitalism, I'm not criticizing the idea of selling things; I'm criticizing the idea that people who have lots of money get to wield power over people who actually work."[27] Same, Mr. Chiang, same.

---

[27] Ted Chiang, "Will A.I. Become the New McKinsey?" The New Yorker, newyorker.com, May 4, 2023.

Labor

As much as I despise Koons (and I really despise Koons, in case you couldn't tell), his method of working, of creating art, is not without historical precedent. Many of the things in our museums, that we now consider art, were made not by the solitary artistic genius, but in workshops or by communities. And I'm not just talking about obvious works, like tapestry weaving. Much painting, even in the Renaissance, which in some eyes birthed the idea of the solitary artistic genius, was a product of the workshop.

Koons is also not the only contemporary artist to get flack for his production methods. Kehinde Wiley - perhaps best known for his official portrait of President Barrack Obama, but in reality, an art world star even before that - has drawn criticism for the revelation that he does not paint all of his massive and intricate paintings himself. It seems that, from big art-world stars to artists skulking in Facebook groups, we struggle with the idea that anyone other than an artist should have a hand in producing a work of art.

Labor

But I think we're asking the wrong question. The question isn't whether or not having someone else make some or part of your work makes it art. The question is, was your work made by exploiting the labor of others? If it was, then that makes it capitalism, not art.

I'll admit that this is a thornier question to answer - much more nuanced and not always easy to discern. Though in the case of Koons, a simple Google search turns up negative reviews from current and former employees, but even those should be taken with a grain of salt. Happy people rarely complain on the Internet. But still, the way Koons seems to use his employees smacks of capitalist exploitation more than anything else.

This question is also difficult to answer for historical pieces. After seeing it mentioned in Etel Adnan's book *Life is a Weaving,* I head to the Musée de Cluny in Paris to see the *Lady and the Unicorn* tapestries. Ok, I didn't just hop over to Paris to see it. I already had a trip planned to Paris when I noticed Adnan's mention of the tapestries and immediately added them to my itinerary. Created around 1500, very little is known about the actual weaving of these works. The speculation is they were produced in a Flemish tapestry workshop, but even that is uncertain. And since we don't know where they were produced, we certainly can't know what kinds of conditions they were produced under. Yet even with this uncertainty, to my eyes, these tapestries are unequivocally art.

But so are Adnan's. A little Internet sleuthing takes me to the website of the company that wove Adnan's work - Maison PINTON. PINTON's website traces its roots back to the traditional French Aubusson tapestry workshops and highlights the skills of its employees. At one point, the website likens the weaving of a tapestry to "the creation of an opera 'where the composer is the artist designing the piece and the conductor is the cartoon painter. He or she adapts the model to the dimensions of the loom. Finally, the musicians are the weavers. They complete the tapestry by

Labor

interpreting the cartoon with colours and shading.'"[28]

Of course, just like with anything else on the Internet, this should be consumed with caution. Corporate propaganda is real, and we can't know for certain the experiences of the weavers working there. This time, my Google search yielded nothing about the working conditions, just some lovely images of hands at work on PINTON's Instagram page.

But this lack of information doesn't change our ability to ask the question. And it doesn't stop us from using it as a metric in our own work and in our own decision to call what we make art. As I told the woman in my group who brought up the question of using assistants to produce your work, the myth of the solitary artistic genius is a myth designed to keep artists poor, while capitalists get rich.

---

[28] "Contemporary Textile Pieces," pinto1867.com, viewed June 27, 2023.

Labor

And I don't mean that as hyperbole. As humans, we have always had a desire for stuff, to surround ourselves with objects filled with beauty and meaning. But capitalism has learned to exploit that desire, turning our love of things into rampant consumerism designed to boost profits through any means necessary - be it labor exploitation or the development of new technologies designed to churn out cheaper and cheaper (but ever more profitable) goods.

Ironically, capitalism's expansion of technology is one of the things that caused art to embrace the myth of the solo creator. In *All About Process,* Kim Grant writes that "Only in the nineteenth century, when industrialization prompted a serious reconsideration of the distinctions between creative and mechanical processes, did the artist's labor in itself become a focus of critical and theoretical concerns."[29]

---

[29] Kim Grant, *All About Process: The Theory and Discourse of Modern Artistic Labor*, University Park: The Pennsylvania State University Press, 2017.

Labor

This comes to play most clearly in Walter Benjamin's famous 1935 essay "The Work of Art in the Age of Mechanical Production" which argues that the soul of art is in the aura, its uniqueness, which can only come from original work. No reproduction, however faithfully it is created, can replicate that aura. If anything can be produced (or reproduced), then it comes down to the soul of the artist and the intent of the creator as the distinguishing factor of what makes something art.

This brings us back to the conundrum of assistants and, for lack of a better term, outsourced production, in the case of tapestry weaving, both historical and contemporary. If the work is made by someone else, does it still retain that aura?

I shudder to think of the things that wouldn't exist if we defined art as only the product of one person's labor. Adnan's tapestries, *The Lady and the Unicorn,* countless other works of art. The world would be poorer without them. And the magic in these pieces doesn't exist because of some

Labor

ambiguous aura. It exists at the crossroads of vision and process, where real human skills come together to create something incredible.

As artists, we limit ourselves when we treat our art as legitimate only if we make it ourselves. For many of us, we have more ideas than we could hope to create in a lifetime, maybe even two lifetimes. The work takes too long and life is too short. There are real advantages to bringing other people along to help execute our vision, most notably in the fact that some work would never get made if we didn't.

This is different from capitalism's goal of producing more and more stuff with the aim of maximizing profit. Yes, creating more work to sell means the potential to make more money as an artist. I'm not denying that fact. And while I am fully in support of artists making money (and not just a little, I think artists contribute immeasurable value to society and should be paid well for that), I also understand that for many artists, money isn't the ultimate goal. The goal is to bring our vision to life, to get our

Labor

ideas (not just conceptual ideas, but those based on a deep sympathy with material and process) out into the world.

One of the arguments in favor of capitalism is that it's the best option we've got. But it doesn't have to be. Capitalism, by its very nature, infers an exploitative relationship between owner and worker. But art doesn't have to follow this path. We can choose to get help (or not) to make our work, but that doesn't mean we have to exploit the people who make it. We can choose to hire or outsource in ethical ways. Creating something for sale, and hiring someone to help us with its production, doesn't automatically make us capitalists, as Chiang argues. The idea of a group of people coming together to create a work of art predates both capitalism and money, though of course not all of those situations were without exploitation.

At the end of the day, the only studio working conditions we can know are our own (or ones we

Labor

are employed in). Hiring assistants to create your work doesn't make you less of an artist and it doesn't negate your work from being art. Just tread wisely. The boundary between whether something is produced as art or whether it's a tool of capitalism has nothing to do with the number of people who came together in service of its creation - instead, it's about the conditions those people labored under and whether or not someone was exploited in the process. Getting assistance doesn't make someone any less of an artist and it doesn't make the output any less art - instead, it's an acknowledgment that collaboration is equally as valid as the life of a solitary artist.

Permission

My friend Sol Proaño and I are standing in front of a mobile by Alexander Calder at the Museum of Modern Art in New York. It is a massive yet airy concoction with spindly arms extending at all angles, including amazingly, elegantly upwards. We are watching it slowly spin when a security guard comes up behind us. "You must have been easily entertained as a child," he jokes. "You've been staring at that for so long. Put a yo-yo in front of you, I bet you would have watched it for hours." It takes me a moment to process this intrusion - Sol and I had been discussing the construction and composition of the mobile, completely lost in our conversation, the way my mom and I used to do at museums - but I finally realize what he is saying

Permission

and stammer "we're artists" with all the conviction I can muster.

"Ah, that explains it," he acknowledges, comprehension dawning on his face. "My daughter is an artist too. She can stay in these exhibitions for a long time." He shakes his head. "Not me." I'll admit that I had a hard time processing why someone who wasn't that interested in art, who didn't have any desire to spend hours in an exhibition, would want to be a security guard in an art museum, but I suppose, for many, a job is a job. And the people-watching is good.

My explanation to the guard - "we're artists" - and his acceptance of it lands on a key reason why any of us would want to claim the title of artist. Being an artist is like having a built-in permission slip. You can linger; in museums, in bars, in cafes, on beaches, in forests, on park benches. You can collect things, squirreling away ideas, materials, books, shells, trash, anything really, all in the hopes of future inspiration or genius. You can act like a child, or an animal, or a total snob, and somehow justify it all under the banner of artist.

In "The Art World," his influential essay from the 1960s, Arthur Danto lists ways an artist, in the vein of Andy Warhol, might engage with a stack of Brillo boxes. The artist could collect them, display them, pile them high, and given the right moment, the right feeling, in the right gallery, someone might praise them as art. But he adds, "we don't say these things about the stockboy."[30] The stockboy, Danto wants to make painfully clear, is not an artist. Danto's reason for this is simple. In his eyes, "a stockroom is not an art gallery."[31]

But does the artist really need an art gallery, when they have permission? Can't a stock person, to update Danto's gendered title, also declare themselves an artist? Why can't the backroom be

---

[30] Arthur Danto, "The Art World," *The Journal of Philosophy*, Vol. 61, No. 19, 1964.

[31] Ibid.

just as much a site for art as the gallery?

Empire Records was my favorite movie in high school. I want to tag onto that statement, in an uncanny impression of one of the movie's antagonists, Rex Manning, "What's your favorite movie now?" and the frightened reply of his fan, "You, still you!" but I know that reference will only endear me to a few hardcore *Empire Record* fans. So back to my main point. This '90s gem chronicles the exploits of a group of misfit indie record store employees as they fight to save their store from the clutches of an evil music store chain. The movie is full of music and randomness and no small amount of teenage drama, and to my young artist self, it was perfect. In one scene, a teen named Warren, in his conspicuously oversized jacket, has been caught shoplifting and made to wait in the store's backroom for the police to arrive. Leaning over from the beat-up couch, he struggles to pick up a quarter that has been affixed to the faded carpet.

Permission

"Who the hell glued these quarters down?" he asks.

"I did," says A.J., the store's resident artist. Oh, A.J. with his slouchy oatmeal-colored cardigan and floppy brown hair and annoying love for Corey, played by Liv Tyler, and his big dreams of becoming an artist. I would have followed A.J. anywhere.

"What the hell for, man?" Warren asks through gritted teeth.

A.J. replies simply, "I don't feel that I need to explain my art to you, Warren."

There it is. Permission.

It matters who gets to call themselves an artist because it is our passport, our ticket, our entrée into a world of unlimited creative expression. It turns any room - a living room, a kitchen, a stockroom, or a gallery - into a site of potential magic. And it should be open to anyone who wants to claim it, not merely those with credentials or who show their work in galleries or end up in museums.

It should be open to illustrators and cartoonists and designers and crafters and anyone else who dares try to take a piece of their heart, their soul, themselves, and turn it into a physical, tangible object.

I think back to William Deresiewicz's comment in *The Death of the Artist* about illustrators and cartoonists and crafters not being artists and my blood boils. For most of us, most of the time, these "non-artists" are our main interaction with art. We don't live in museums, we live in the real world. But that world isn't any less full of art, or at least, it doesn't have to be.

Children's books are often the first way that many people are introduced to art. I read *Dr. Seuss's ABCs* so many times as a child that the spine disintegrated and my mother had to purchase a new copy for my three younger siblings. And while I am less likely to purchase a Dr. Seuss book these days, there's no denying the impact those books and many others had on my childhood. I have made every attempt to pass on this love of art, and reading, to my niblings (my siblings' children), buying them children's books since before they were born, and sending them illustrated books throughout the pandemic, hoping it would keep them entertained without screens and give their parents a few minutes of, if not rest, at least relieved pressure from having to come up with yet another thing for the kids to do in quarantine.

I also send them art supplies. I'll admit that I not so secretly want one or more of my niblings to grow up to be artists. If not artists, I will at least settle for art lovers, and so I fill their shelves with books on Frida Kahlo and Yayoi Kusama and Ruth Asawa and Claude Monet and Henri Matisse and Zaha Hadid. And I send them stories beautifully illustrated by Kenesha Sneed and Julie Morstad and Oliver

Permission

Jeffers and Owen Davey and Danielle Krysa and Christopher Silas Neal. These illustrators may not be as famous as the artists who grace our museums, but their art is valuable nonetheless.

But truthfully, I want my niblings to become artists. Not necessarily artists who go to art school, or aspire to exhibit in galleries or museums, or who even necessarily make art regularly. I want them to be artists because I want them to have permission to approach the world like an artist.

I want them to linger, not just in galleries and museums, but in bookstores and on beaches and in forests, and in the homes of their friends and family. I want them to see the world with fascination and wonder and awe. I want them to collect things, not because someone said those things are valuable, but because those things make them feel something - beauty, fascination, repulsion, something, anything. And I want them to weave the act of artful creation into every moment of their lives, whether that's at home, in a gallery, or in a stockroom.

And I want that for you too. There are a lot of reasons to call yourself an artist, but the most important is that it lets you approach the world in a different way. Being an artist gives you permission to do things that other people would only dream about.

And that can be scary.

We have been taught that to be an artist is to be self-indulgent. This is the concept of genius Clare Dederer shares in *Monsters*. The great artist is, to look at Picasso or Pollock, an asshole, but it's justified because the work is great. (For the record, I'm not saying the work is great. I'm saying that's how it's perceived by many.) But most of us don't want to be assholes. We don't even want to be geniuses. We just want the time and space to create our work.

Permission

And because we don't want to be assholes, we spend an enormous amount of time and energy worrying about what people think of us. But this time and energy spent worrying depletes our ability to approach the world as artists.

In a talk at the Alt Summit conference a number of years ago, the artist Lisa Congdon shared an idea that is both simple and profound: "You can be an enormously caring person and not care what people think about you." It immediately struck me, because it perfectly described someone I knew so well.

That person was my mother.

It wasn't only in making art that my mother solidified her identity as an artist. She understood that to be an artist meant seeking out art, finding inspiration, and living a full life, on your own terms. She embraced travel and books and made time to both make and seek out art.

Permission

All of this - her commitment to her art practice, her books, her love of art-related travel, and of course, the art itself - added up to a certainty that, whether she received money for it or not, my mother was indeed an artist. But it was also her approach to life that made her an artist. She carried that "I don't give a fuck attitude" that we associate with the most self-assured, confident artists. She made time to make and seek out art. But she wasn't an asshole. She cared very deeply about the people, the things, the world around her. She approached the world like an artist, excited about everything it had to offer, and always willing to share that excitement with the people around her.

She cared about life, about art, about people, but she didn't give a fuck what people thought about her. That is the power of giving yourself permission to be an artist.

The MOMA guard walks back to his post, but as Sol and I round the room toward where he is standing, he stops us again. "Are either of you actually

Permission

sculptors?" I am almost as startled by this question as I am by his first comment but respond quickly. "Actually, yes, we both are. We both make jewelry..." "That's sculpture," he interjects quickly, in case we needed reassurance before I continue, "but we both also make sculpture." I am thinking of Sol's gorgeous pieces, hangings and tabletop sculptures with brass wire and prisms that scatter rainbows as they catch the light, and my own sculptures, riots of welded wire floral patterns formed to look like chairs and pillows, all completely unusable, made in graduate school and the years after, before I turned my attention back to jewelry. I'm not exactly sure why I feel the need to justify this, to justify us. It's almost as if I want to assert our position - we too, belong here, in this art world.

But the guard continues, his face full of pride, and I realize my justifications are unnecessary. "That's great," he replies. "My daughter is an illustrator."

Acknowledgments

Many of the words in this book took various forms before ending up here and I am eternally grateful to everyone who read whole or parts of this writing, and who helped shape this book into what it became.

I'm also grateful to my family, who have always supported my decision to be an artist, even when I didn't call myself one.

And I'm especially thankful to all the artists and makers I have met over the years - those who talked to me at conferences or who took my classes, particularly the members of my online coaching program, Artists & Profit Makers. Your willingness to be vulnerable - to share your doubts and fears along with your hopes and dreams - is what motivated me to write this book. Thank you.

Selected Bibliography

Arkhipov, Vladimir, *Home-Made Europe: Contemporary Folk Artifacts,* London: Fuel, 2006.

Auther, Elissa, "The Decorative, Abstraction, and the Hierarchy of Art and Craft in the Art Criticism of Clement Greenberg," Oxford Art Journal, Vol. 27, No. 3, 2004.

Chapman, Jonathan, *Emotionally Durable Design: Objects, Experiences and Empathy*, Oxfordshire: Routledge, 2015.

Danto, Arthur, "The Art World," *The Journal of Philosophy,* Vol. 61, No. 19, 1964.

de Botton, Alain and John Armstrong, *Art as Therapy*, London: Phaidon Press, 2016.

Dederer, Claire, *Monsters: A Fan's Dilemma*, London: Scepter, 2023

Deresiewicz, William, *The Death of the Artist: How Creators Are Struggling to Survive in the Age of Billionaires and Big Tech*, New York: Henry Holt, 2020.

Grant, Kim, *All About Process: The Theory and Discourse of Modern Artistic Labor*, University Park: The Pennsylvania State University Press, 2017.

Moss, Hugh, *The Art of Understanding Art: A New Perspective,* London: Profile Books, 2015.

Paz, Octavio, "Seeing and Using: Art and Craftsmanship" from *Convergences: Essays on Art and Literature*, San Diego: Harcourt Brace Jovanovich, Inc, 1987.

Proctor, Alice, *The Whole Picture: The Colonial History of Art in Our Museums*, London: Cassell, 2020.

Reed, Christopher, *Not at Home: The Suppression of Domesticity in Modern Art and Architecture*, London: Thames and Hudson, 1996.

Singerman, Howard, *Art Subjects: Making Artists in the American University,* Berkeley: University of California Press, 1999.

Swinth, Kirsten, *Painting Professionals: Women Artists and the Development of Modern American Art, 1870-1930*, Chapel Hill: The University of North Carolina Press, 2001.

About the Author

Megan Auman is an artist, metalsmith, writer, educator, and creative business coach. She has a BFA from Syracuse University and an MFA from Kent State University, but neither of those are what makes her an artist. She lives and works in Jonestown, Pennsylvania, a small town ninety miles west of Philly, in a house and studio filled with books, plants, and art. *Permission to Be an Artist* is her fourth book.

To learn more, visit meganauman.com

www.ingramcontent.com/pod-product-compliance
Lightning Source LLC
Chambersburg PA
CBHW071417210526
45465CB00001B/428